MINDSET MATTERS

10 BEST MINDSETS FOR SELF-IMPROVEMENT

MANJUNATHA A R

NOTION PRESS

Published by
Notion Press Media Pvt Ltd,
#7, Red Cross Road,
Egmore, Chennai, Tamil Nadu 600008

Book title: MINDSET MATTERS
Subtitle: 10 Best Mindsets For Self-Improvement

ISBN XXX-X-XXXXXXX-X-X

First Impression Feb 2024
The moral right of the author has been asserted.
This edition is for sale in the Indian subcontinent only.

Printed in India

Ordering Information
Quantity sales. Special discounts are available on quantity
purchases by corporations, associations, and others. For details,
contact the publisher at the address above.

NOTION PRESS

India. Singapore. Malaysia.

ISBN- XXX-X-XXXXXXX-X-X

Contents

At Lotus feet of Acharya Chanakya

Prologue

In life's adventure, our perspective plays a role in shaping our experiences, choices and results. It serves as the filter through which we see the world and the motivating factor behind our actions. This book delves into ten ways of Mindset that can truly transform our lives and unlock our potential. From the Growth Mindset, which embraces challenges as opportunities for growth, to the Action Mindset, which propels us to take strategic steps towards our goals, each Mindset provides valuable insights and practical strategies for achieving success and fulfilment. Whether you desire to cultivate resilience, welcome abundance into your life or courageously pursue your dreams, these mindsets serve as guiding principles that empower and inspire you on your journey.

Join us as we explore the depths of psychology, investigating how Mindset can be a catalyst for transformation while discovering the keys to unlocking a passionate and prosperous life. Let this book serve as your roadmap towards development as you embark on a voyage of self-discovery and empowerment guided by these ten mindsets of revolutionizing your existence.

- **[*Globetrotting_Urban Saint*]**

Place: Vijaynagar, Mysore

Date: 13/02/2024

****

"Failure isn't the end of the road; it's just a detour on the path to success."

- A.R

"Feedback is the compass that guides us towards improvement, leading us closer to our best selves."

- Globetrotting_Urban Saint

Growth Mindset

****

A growth mindset means believing one can develop one's abilities and intelligence with dedication and hard work.

People with a growth mindset acknowledge that talents and intelligence are not fixed characteristics but can nurtured over time.

They welcome challenges and see failures as chances to learn and persevere when faced with setbacks.

Key characteristics of a growth mindset include:

1. Embracing Challenges:

Overall, cultivating a growth mindset involves fostering a belief in the power of effort, resilience, and continuous learning. By adopting this Mindset, individuals can unlock their full potential and succeed in various aspects of their lives. Adopting a growth mindset means embracing challenges as opportunities for professional growth.

Individuals with this Mindset view obstacles as roadblocks and use them as milestones towards success.

They don't shy away from difficulties. Face them with determination and resilience, recognizing that each challenge offers a chance to learn, adapt and improve.

A vital characteristic of those with a growth mindset is their willingness to step outside their comfort zones. Then, sticking to what's familiar and safe, they actively seek challenges that push their limits and help them grow. They believe in the power of development. Understand that progress often requires venturing into uncharted territory.

In addition, people with a growth mindset approach challenges with an attitude and curiosity. Instead of considering setbacks and failures, they perceive them as feedback that helps refine their strategies and develop new skills. This optimistic outlook allows them to stay motivated in the face of adversity.

Furthermore, individuals who embrace a growth mindset recognize mastery as a journey rather than a final destination.

They understand that growth is a journey that demands dedication and effort. Instead of getting discouraged by setbacks or obstacles, they see them as integral parts of the learning process.

In essence, embracing challenges goes beyond overcoming difficulties; it entails embracing the path of self-exploration and personal development. By facing challenges, individuals with a growth mindset develop resilience, perseverance and a profound sense of satisfaction as they work towards unlocking their capabilities.

2. Viewing Failure as Feedback:

Seeing failure as a form of feedback is an aspect of fostering a growth mindset.

Then, allowing setbacks to determine their worth or capabilities, individuals who embrace a growth mindset understand that failure is a part of the learning journey.

They view failure as a source of feedback and understanding. When confronted with failure, those with a growth mindset approach the situation with curiosity and openness, reflect on what went wrong, and carefully examine the circumstances and their actions. By analyzing their mistakes, they gain insights into areas where they can improve and develop.

Moreover, individuals with a growth mindset recognize that failure is not permanent but an obstacle.

They maintain optimism and resilience, knowing that setbacks are opportunities for growth and progress. Of dwelling on failures, they find motivation in them to persistently work towards their goals.

Additionally, those with a growth mindset actively seek feedback from others because they understand that external perspectives can provide insights and different viewpoints. They welcome criticism. Use it as an instrument for self-improvement. By integrating feedback into their learning process, they continuously refine their skills. Enhance their abilities.

Essentially, considering failure as a form of feedback involves a change in Mindset that empowers people to approach challenges and setbacks with resilience and determination.

When individuals with a growth mindset reframe failure as a chance for development, they can overcome obstacles.

Attain higher levels of success in various aspects of their lives, personal or professional.

3. Persistence and Resilience:

Persistence and resilience are elements of a growth mindset that set individuals who possess this Mindset apart from those who may give up on challenges. Of seeing setbacks as obstacles, people with a growth mindset approach difficulties with a determination to persevere and the ability to bounce back from adversity.

A critical aspect of persistence is the commitment to effort and hard work.

Those with a growth mindset understand that achieving goals requires dedication over time; rather than getting discouraged by challenges, they stay focused on their objectives and consistently put in the necessary work to make progress.

Resilience involves the capacity to recover from setbacks and adapt to changing circumstances. When faced with failures or difficulties, individuals with a growth mindset don't let these challenges define them. Instead, they learn from their experiences, adjust their strategies and use setbacks as opportunities for development.

The combination of persistence and resilience empowers individuals with a growth mindset to navigate life's ups and downs. They don't see obstacles as reasons to give up on their pursuits; instead, they view them as chances to refine their approach, learn lessons, and become even more vital.

Moreover, those with a growth mindset tend to perceive challenges not as threats but as opportunities for demonstrating their resilience.

They know that facing challenges helps them develop their character, improve their skills and contribute to their growth.

Having perseverance and resilience motivates people to stay dedicated to their goals and show resilience when faced with difficulties.

4. Seeking Feedback and Criticism:

Seeking feedback and criticism is a behaviour for people with a growth mindset.

Those with a growth mindset acknowledge that they do not possess all the answers and that there is always room for progress...

As a result, they proactively seek input from others, appreciating perspectives and insights that can help them identify blind spots, areas for growth and opportunities to enhance their abilities. Individuals with a growth mindset view feedback with an attitude and a genuine desire to learn. They comprehend that constructive criticism is not an attack on their character but rather an opportunity to gain perspectives and insights. Rather than becoming defensive or discouraged by feedback, they view it as a gift that can aid their evolution.

Moreover, people with a growth mindset actively solicit feedback from colleagues, mentors, supervisors, and customers or clients. They recognize that each perspective offers a viewpoint through which they can evaluate their performance and behaviour more comprehensively—enabling them to understand their strengths and areas requiring improvement. Additionally, those with a growth mindset fully embrace the concept of enhancement. Actively look for opportunities to receive feedback, regularly checking in with others to assess their progress and get input on improving their skills and abilities.

In essence, seeking feedback and accepting criticism is the behaviour of individuals with a growth mindset. By embracing feedback as a learning and personal development tool, they show their dedication to continuously improving and their willingness to push themselves to reach their potential.

5. Celebrating Effort and Progress:

In a growth mindset, the focus shifts from fixed ideas about talent or intelligence to recognizing the value of effort and progress. People who adopt this Mindset appreciate the growth journey, understanding that success is not solely determined by abilities but by dedication and perseverance.

One of the aspects of appreciating effort and progress involves acknowledging the significance of work. By attributing success to talent or luck, individuals with a growth mindset acknowledge the role of effort in attaining their goals. They take pride in the work they invest in, such as studying into the night, repeatedly practising a skill, or facing challenges with determination.

Furthermore, individuals with a growth mindset comprehend the importance of improvements. Then, focusing on significant accomplishments, they value each small step forward they take along their journey. Whether mastering a concept, achieving a goal, or overcoming a fear, they celebrate each milestone as evidence of their ongoing growth and development.

Moreover, those embracing a growth mindset foster an environment of encouragement and support for themselves and others. They understand that progress doesn't always follow a path and that setbacks are natural during learning processes.

Then, dwelling on failures or shortcomings, individuals concentrate on their accomplishments and view setbacks as opportunities for introspection and personal development.

Moreover, those with a growth mindset surround themselves with individuals who share their values and beliefs. They actively seek mentors, coaches and peers who will support them while challenging them to reach their potential. Fostering a community that promotes encouragement and accountability creates an environment where effort and progress are cherished and esteemed.

Essentially, celebrating effort and progress is an aspect of adopting a growth mindset. By shifting the focus from abilities to the significance of dedication and perseverance, individuals embracing this Mindset cultivate a sense of pride and fulfilment in their journey of personal growth and self-improvement.

***

Gratitude Mindset.

****

A gratitude mindset entails adopting a perspective that focuses on recognizing and valuing the multitude of blessings in our lives, regardless of their size. It involves nurturing a sense of appreciation and acknowledging the elements within our experiences, relationships and situations.

Key characteristics of a gratitude mindset include:

1. Focus on the Present:

People who adopt a mindset of gratitude understand the importance of living in the moment and finding happiness and satisfaction in the joys of everyday life. By practising mindfulness and being fully aware, they develop a sense of gratitude for the aspects of their current reality.

An essential aspect of embracing the Present is engaging in practices. Those with a gratitude mindset consciously try to slow down and appreciate their surroundings, whether savouring a cup of tea in the morning, taking walks amidst nature or cherishing quality time spent with loved ones.

Furthermore, individuals with a gratitude mindset actively seek opportunities to cultivate gratefulness throughout their lives. They reflect on things they're thankful for regardless of their size or significance—and express appreciation for the blessings they have received. By focusing on the moment and recognizing abundance in their lives, they nurture contentment and fulfilment that goes beyond material possessions or external accomplishments.

Moreover, people with a gratitude mindset approach challenges and setbacks with resilience and optimism. Then, dwelling on regrets or worrying about what lies ahead, they concentrate on the current moment and view it as an opportunity for personal growth and learning. By staying grounded in the here and now, individuals become more adept at navigating the highs and lows of life with poise and serenity.

Moreover, those who embrace a mindset of gratitude foster a sense of interconnectedness with the world around them. Appreciates the beauty and marvels found in moments—children's laughter or the breathtaking sight of a sunset—and harbour profound gratitude for the intricate tapestry of existence that sustains them.

In essence, directing one's focus on the moment constitutes a practice that empowers individuals embracing gratitude to encounter heightened joy, fulfilment and well-being. By nurturing mindfulness and acknowledging the richness, they unlock happiness and contentment at their core in every passing second.

2. Counting Blessings:

Recognizing and appreciating the abundance in our lives is a practice known as counting blessings. It's all acknowledging and expressing gratitude for the many blessings, big and small, that contribute to our well-being and happiness.

A crucial aspect of counting blessings is developing awareness and mindfulness of the aspects of life. Those who engage in this practice take time daily to reflect on things they're grateful for. It could be the love and support from family and friends, good health, fulfilling work or even the little joys that bring happiness to their day.

Counting blessings involves expressing gratitude for the richness of experiences and connections that add value to one's life, including appreciating nature's beauty, a smile from a stranger, acts of kindness received or shared, or moments filled with laughter among loved ones. By recognizing and cherishing these experiences, individuals cultivate a sense of appreciation and contentment that contributes to their well-being. Focusing on what's lacking or going wrong, people redirect their attention towards the abundance of blessings surrounding them.

Moreover, individuals who regularly take stock of their blessings often undergo shifts in their perspective and attitude. They develop a sense of gratitude and humility, acknowledging the interconnectedness of all things and the importance of expressing appreciation for the gifts they have received. This attitude of gratitude not only brings joy and fulfilment into their lives but inspires others to cultivate a similar mindset of appreciation and abundance.

Counting blessings is a practice that nurtures a sense of gratitude, connection and well-being. By recognizing and expressing thanks for the abundance in their lives, individuals foster an outlook and an increased capacity for joy, resilience and contentment.

3. Shifting Perspective:
By shifting their thoughts towards gratitude, individuals change their perspective from scarcity to abundance.

Cherish the small blessings surrounding them each day, such as the support of loved ones, the beauty of nature moments filled with joy and laughter, or even the simple pleasures of everyday life.

This shift in perspective fosters a sense of contentment and satisfaction as individuals learn to view their lives through a lens of appreciation rather than comparison or longing. Then, striving for more or feeling inadequate, they find fulfilment in the present moment and the richness of their experiences.

Furthermore, embracing a mindset of gratitude can help individuals navigate challenges and setbacks with resilience and optimism. They become skilled at finding silver linings and opportunities for growth during times. Ultimately, adopting an outlook can have an impact on our lives. Shifting our focus towards acknowledging the abundance of blessings and fixating on what we lack allows us to experience a profound sense of gratitude and happiness.

***

Resilience Mindset

****

The Mindset of resilience provides individuals with a framework to navigate the challenges and setbacks that arise in life. It equips them with strength, adaptability and determination. Let's explore each component in detail to understand how individuals cultivate resilience;

1. Maintaining Perspective: Resilience entails maintaining a viewpoint when faced with setbacks and adversity. While acknowledging their challenges, resilient individuals comprehend that these setbacks are temporary and do not define their worth or potential. They maintain a long-term outlook on their goals, understanding that perseverance is crucial for success.

EX: Consider a student grappling with challenges in college. While facing difficulties in a course, they maintain a balanced perspective by recognizing that one setback does not determine their academic abilities or potential for growth. Of fixating on their weaknesses, they reach out to tutors and professors for assistance, recognizing that temporary setbacks are a part of the learning journey and do not hinder their ultimate goal of graduating with honours.

2. Nurturing Adaptability: Being adaptable is a characteristic of resilience. Resilient individuals are flexible and open to change, capable of adjusting their strategies and goals in response to shifting circumstances. They view uncertainty as opportunities for growth and innovation, finding solutions to overcome challenges.

EX: An employee navigating an evolving work environment serves as an example of adaptability. When confronted with technologies or organizational changes, they embrace these transformations as chances to expand their skills and adapt to responsibilities. They remain flexible and receptive to quickly learning systems and processes to stay relevant and valuable within their team.

3. Establishing Supportive Networks: Resilience thrives within relationships. Resilient individuals cultivate connections with friends, family members, mentors and colleagues who offer support, encouragement and practical assistance during challenging times. These networks become sources of strength and resilience during periods.

An individual facing a crisis such as loss or illness exemplifies the significance of support networks. They rely on the support of their loved ones, such as friends, family and support groups, to provide guidance and practical help. By surrounding themselves with caring individuals who offer encouragement and understanding, they find the strength and resilience to navigate through times.

4. Taking Care of Self: Self-care is crucial for maintaining resilience. Resilient people prioritize their emotional and mental well-being by participating in activities that promote relaxation, stress management and self-reflection. They understand the importance of replenishing their energy levels to cope with challenges and bounce back from setbacks effectively.

EX: Consider a professional who has demanding work obligations alongside family responsibilities. Despite their schedule, they prioritize self-care by engaging in exercise, meditation and hobbies that bring them joy and relaxation. They replenish their energy levels by dedicating time to recharge and nurture their well-being. Maintain resilience when faced with stressors or adversity.

5. Learning from Challenges: Resilient individuals see challenges as opportunities for growth. They reflect on setbacks, identify areas for development and use these experiences as lessons to guide actions and decisions. Adversity catalyzes growth and self-discovery—leading to increased resilience and wisdom.

EX: An athlete recovering from an injury that could have ended their career is a shining example of resilience in the face of adversity. Instead of giving up on their dreams of being an athlete, they view this setback as a chance for self-reflection and personal growth. They dedicate themselves to rehabilitation, learning the importance of patience, perseverance and resilience. Ultimately, they make a comeback to their sport even stronger and more determined.

6. Maintaining a Positive Outlook: Optimism plays a role in fostering resilience. Individuals who possess resilience maintain a perspective. Believe in their ability to overcome challenges even when faced with adversity. They nurture hope, confidence and resilience within themselves by relying on both their strength and external support systems to persist and thrive.

EX: Lastly, let's consider how communities come together after disasters. Despite experiencing loss and devastation, they hold onto optimism. Hope for the future. Drawing strength from one another, they unite to rebuild homes and livelihoods by providing support and assistance. By emphasizing the strength of their community and embracing opportunities for renewal, they embody optimism and resilience in the face of adversity.

To sum it up, having a mindset is an encompassing approach to gracefully navigating life challenges with determination, embracing difficulties, keeping an outlook, being flexible, forming connections with others, taking care of oneself, gaining wisdom from setbacks and staying hopeful people can develop resilience and flourish when confronted with challenges.

***

Purpose Mindset

****

Living with a purpose-oriented mindset means acknowledging and embracing a sense of purpose while ensuring that our actions align with our values and beliefs. It involves recognizing our strengths, passions and aspirations and directing them towards goals and endeavours. People who adopt a purpose-driven mindset seek fulfilment and guidance by pursuing activities and commitments that resonate with their purpose.

Let's take a look at the elements of the purpose-driven Mindset;

1. Clarity of Purpose: Individuals who embrace a purpose-oriented mindset understand what matters to them. They take the time to reflect on their values, passions and long-term objectives, gaining clarity about their mission or purpose. This clarity is a guiding compass for making decisions and taking actions that keep them focused and aligned with their purpose.

2. Alignment with Values: Living with a purpose-oriented mindset requires aligning our actions and behaviours with our core values and beliefs. We consciously make choices that reflect our values, whether they pertain to relationships, career decisions, or lifestyle choices.

By staying committed to their core values, individuals experience a sense of integrity and genuineness in their actions, resulting in increased satisfaction and fulfilment.

3. Meaningful Engagement: People with a purpose-oriented mindset actively seek opportunities for involvement.

They pursue activities, projects and relationships that resonate with their sense of purpose, finding joy and fulfilment in impacting others or contributing to causes they deeply care about. Whether it involves volunteering for an organization, choosing a career that aligns with their passions or fostering connections with loved ones, they prioritize engagements that add significance and purpose to their lives.

4. Impact and Contribution: Individuals embracing a purpose-oriented mindset are motivated to create an impact and contribute to something more. They acknowledge their unique strengths and talents as assets to serve others or work towards objectives. Through endeavours, volunteer work, artistic pursuits or acts of kindness, they strive to leave a lasting legacy and improve the world.

In general, embracing a purpose-driven mindset ensures that our actions align with our values, passions and sense of purpose. This approach allows us to lead a prosperous life in significance and fulfilment and make contributions. It involves living with intentionality, understanding who we are, and dedicating ourselves to positively impacting the world.

***

Abundance Mindset

****

The abundance mindset is a way of thinking that revolves around believing in the abundance of possibilities and opportunities available to everyone. It involves nurturing a mindset of abundance rather than scarcity, focusing on what can be gained or lacking. Those who adopt the abundance mindset approach life with optimism, gratitude, and empowerment. They view challenges as chances for growth and success.

Here's a deeper exploration of the abundance mindset;

1. Optimism and Positivity: Individuals with an abundant mindset maintain a perspective on life. They firmly believe that good things are not only possible but abundant. They perceive setbacks as temporary. See challenges as opportunities for personal development and learning. This positive outlook allows them to face life with enthusiasm, resilience and confidence in overcoming obstacles.

2. Gratitude and Appreciation: Gratitude forms the foundation of an abundance mindset. Those who embrace this way of thinking cultivate a sense of appreciation for the blessings in their lives, whether it's relationships, good health, fulfilling work or simple joys. By focusing on what they have rather than what they lack, they attract abundance into their lives and experience greater happiness and fulfilment.

3. Empowerment and Taking Control: The abundance mindset allows individuals to take charge of their lives and shape their desired outcomes.

Of feeling like victims of circumstances, they acknowledge their ability to influence their reality through thoughts, beliefs and actions.

This sense of control empowers them to pursue their goals confidently and persistently, knowing they can make their dreams come true.

4. Embracing Opportunities: Embodying the abundance mindset involves being receptive to possibilities and opportunities. Individuals with this Mindset maintain a perspective of abundance rather than scarcity, firmly believing there's more than enough for everyone. This openness enables them to seize opportunities as they present themselves in professional domains, approaching experiences with curiosity and excitement.

5. Generosity and an Abundance Philosophy: Those who embrace an abundance mindset operate from a place of generosity and a philosophy rooted in plenty.

Instead of hoarding resources or competing against others, they embrace the notion that there's success, wealth, and happiness for all to share.

This mentality promotes collaboration, cooperation and a sense of community, leading to prosperity and well-being. Essentially, having an abundance mindset means adopting an outlook that allows individuals to perceive the world as brimming with possibilities and opportunities. Individuals can tap into their potential by nurturing optimism, gratitude, empowerment, openness and generosity. Craft a life filled with abundance, fulfilment and happiness.

***

You Have a Choice Mindset

****

The "You Have a Choice" mindset is quite different from the fixed Mindset, which is the belief that individuals have limited control over their lives and circumstances. In a fixed mindset, people view their abilities, intelligence and potential as traits that cannot be developed or altered.

Here's how the "You Always Have a Choice" mindset contrasts with the fixed Mindset;

1. Personal Empowerment vs Helplessness: The "You Have a Choice" mindset emphasizes empowerment and highlights the belief that individuals can shape their lives through choices and actions. In contrast, the fixed Mindset fosters feelings of helplessness, where individuals believe that external factors or innate characteristics determine their outcomes, leaving them lacking control.

2. Accountability vs. Blame: Individuals adopting the "You Always Have a Choice" Mindset take accountability for their thoughts, emotions and actions. They recognize that they have control over how they respond to situations, accept responsibility for their decisions, and how those decisions impact their lives. Conversely, those with a fixed mindset often blame circumstances or others for their shortcomings or failures, avoiding responsibility and inhibiting personal growth.

3. Empowerment vs Limitation: The "You Have a Choice" mindset empowers individuals and boosts their self-confidence. It encourages them to take charge of their lives and make decisions that align with their values and aspirations. On the other hand, a fixed mindset creates a sense of limitation and resignation where individuals feel confined by their perceived lack of ability or control, leading to frustration, stagnation and unfulfilled potential.

4. Mindful Decision-Making vs. Reactive Responses: Individuals with the "You Always Have a Choice" mindset practice decision-making. They pause to consider their options and choose responses that align with their long-term goals and values. They approach challenges with resilience and determination, seeking opportunities for growth and learning. In contrast, those with a fixed mindset often react impulsively or habitually to situations driven by fear, doubt or the belief that they have no control over their destiny.

5. Freedom vs. Limitation: Ultimately, the "You Have a Choice" mindset liberates individuals from feeling trapped or limited by their circumstances. It reminds them that they can interpret events in ways that allow them to choose how they respond emotionally and take actions that move them forward. On the other hand, having a fixed mindset can make you feel limited and resigned, as if external forces are in control. You have no say in shaping your future.

To sum it up, adopting a "You Have a Choice" mindset empowers individuals to take charge of their lives, make decisions and bring about positive changes. Conversely, the fixed Mindset perpetuates feelings of helplessness, limitations and resignation. By embracing agency, taking responsibility for one's actions, finding empowerment, making choices and cherishing freedom, individuals can break free from the constraints of a fixed mindset and live with greater purposefulness, resilience and fulfilment.

***

Let it Go Mindset

****

The Mindset of "Let It Go" emphasizes the significance of accepting, detachment and releasing control over things beyond our influence. It involves understanding the inevitability of change and recognizing that *holding onto attachments, expectations, or regrets only leads to suffering.* Instead, individuals who adopt this Mindset choose to let go of the past, relinquish their need for control and live in the moment with a sense of freedom and openness.

1. Embracing the Dance of Change: Envision life as a captivating dance where everything moves gracefully and changes fluidly. In this dance, individuals with a "Let It Go" Mindset are like dancers who effortlessly glide across the floor, embracing each step and movement with joy and acceptance. They comprehend that the beauty of dance lies in its evolution and flow; hence, they choose to release expectations and allow life's music to guide them.

2. Painting with the Colors of Surrender: Imagine life as a canvas that needs to be painted with colours symbolizing surrender. Those who embrace the "Let It Go" Mindset resemble master artists who dip their brushes into palettes filled with acceptance and letting go. With every brushstroke, they create awe-inspiring landscapes that exude tranquillity and serenity. They release the need to control every minutiae, allowing the painting to evolve naturally.

3. Navigating Life Waves, with Detachment: Visualize life as an ocean, where waves of change gracefully roll in. Individuals who embrace the "Let It Go" Mindset are like sailors skillfully manoeuvring their ships through the ebb and flow of tides. They raise their sails high, fearlessly embracing the winds of change with grace, surrendering to the rhythm of waves, trusting in the journey and finding solace in the sea.

4. Constructing Fortresses of Forgiveness on Sandy Shores: Envision life as a beach where time erases footprints from the past. Those who possess the "Let It Go" Mindset are akin to architects crafting fortresses built on forgiveness along their heart's shoreline. With each wave of forgiveness, they release resentment and bitterness, allowing times sands to heal wounds and restore harmony within their souls.

5. Engaging in a Dance with Grateful Fireflies: Imagine life as a forest illuminated by firefly flickers at night. People with the "Let It Go" mentality resemble dancers twirling and spinning in the glow of gratitude. With each movement, they let go of the weight of worries and regrets, embracing the beauty of the present moment and finding happiness in life's simple marvels.

6. Taking Flight with Surrender: Visualize life as a sky, where clouds of uncertainty leisurely drift across the horizon. Those who adopt the "Let It Go" Mindset are akin to fearless birds spreading their wings and soaring high above those clouds. With each flap of their wings, they release the urge to control or manipulate, surrendering themselves to the winds of change and trusting in forces that propel them forward.

7. Cultivating Acceptance: Picture life as a garden brimming with growth and rejuvenation. Individuals who embody the "Let It Go" Mindset are like gardeners nurturing their soul's soil. By planting seeds of acceptance, they let go of perfectionism and control while allowing transformative changes to take root and blossom into flowers representing resilience and inner peace.

In conclusion, adopting a "Let It Go" mentality encourages individuals to embrace life with creativity, imagination, and awe. By embracing the magnificence of the moment, letting go of attachments and having faith, individuals nurture a profound feeling of serenity, liberation and happiness in the rhythm of life. This perspective enables them to navigate life's shifting terrain gracefully and resiliently, discovering beauty and motivation in each passing instant.

***

Civil Engineer Mindset

****

The transformative Mindset is a perspective that encourages growth, evolution and positive change. It involves adopting a transformation mindset, where individuals actively seek opportunities to improve themselves, learn, and develop. People with a mindset are open to experiences, different viewpoints and possibilities. They approach life with curiosity, resilience and a willingness to push their limits.

Now, let's dive deeper into the components of the Mindset;

1. Building Bridges for Change: Visualize life as a landscape with rivers and valleys connected through progress bridges. Imagine engineers as agents of change who design these bridges to bridge the gap between challenges and solutions. With each blueprint they create, they seize the chance to build connections that transform communities and create paths for growth and prosperity.

2. Constructing Foundations of Resilience: Envision life as a construction site where the foundations of resilience are laid amid circumstances. Picture civil engineers as builders who fortify structures with the strength to withstand adversities like storms. With each reinforcement they make, they perceive change as an opportunity to strengthen society's foundations and shape a future for future generations.

3. Designing Skyscrapers of Innovation: Imagine a cityscape where towering skyscrapers reach for the sky, representing a vision of innovation. Civil engineers, with a mindset, play the role of architects designing buildings that push the boundaries of what is possible. With every blueprint they create, they embrace the challenge of change by incorporating cutting-edge technologies and sustainable practices, ultimately shaping cities that inspire wonder and shape our future.

4. Paving Roads to Progress: Envision a network of roads spanning landscapes symbolizing progress and opportunity. Civil engineers with a transformative mindset are like pioneers of progress, paving roads that lead to new horizons of growth and development. With each mile laid down, they perceive change as an opportunity to chart paths and connect communities, creating bridges that bridge the gaps between dreams and accomplishments.

5. Harvesting Renewable Resources of Creativity: Visualize life as a landscape of untapped natural resources waiting to be utilized. Civil engineers with a mindset take on the role of sustainability guardians, harvesting creative resources to fuel progress engines. With each solution they develop, they see change as an opening to nature's forces in service and to society—creating sustainable solutions that preserve our planet for future generations.

6. Empowering Communities through Empowerment: Imagine a tapestry comprising the bonds of community and collaboration. With a mindset, civil engineers act as agents of empowerment, uplifting communities by developing infrastructure that fosters connection and opens doors to opportunities. With each project they undertake, they embrace change as a chance to empower individuals and enhance their quality of life, creating environments that nurture growth and prosperity.

7. Navigating Challenges with Flexibility: Visualize life as a meandering river flowing through landscapes filled with challenges and transformations. Civil engineers with a mindset are like navigators charting courses that adapt to the currents of change. In every project they take on, they welcome change as a part of the journey, navigating obstacles with flexibility and resilience to ensure progress continues to move.

In conclusion, having a transformative mindset empowers civil engineers to see change as an opportunity for innovation, collaboration, and the creation of solutions that positively shape our world. By embracing resilience, sustainability, and empowerment, civil engineers pave the path for communities to thrive while using infrastructure as a catalyst for transformation.

***

Get Out Mindset

****

The "Get Out" Mindset is an approach that empowers individuals to break free from their comfort zones, negative thinking patterns, self-imposed limitations, scarcity mindset and anything else that hinders their path to success and fulfilment. It's about embracing change, taking steps and seizing opportunities with unwavering determination and resilience.

1. Stepping Beyond Comfort Zones: The "Get Out" Mindset challenges individuals to step outside the boundaries of what feels familiar and safe. It encourages them to explore territories where growth and transformation thrive. By pushing their limits and embracing discomfort, individuals with this Mindset unlock levels of potential and discover untapped possibilities.

2. Conquering Negativity: Those who embrace the "Get Out" Mindset refuse to be burdened by negativity. They confront pessimism, doubt and self-criticism head-on while cultivating optimism, self-belief and a can-do attitude. They create a momentum that propels them forward by focusing on solutions or dwelling on problems.

3. Breaking Free from Limiting Beliefs: Limiting beliefs act as chains that restrain individuals from reaching their potential or experiencing progress."The Mindset of breaking liberates individuals from these chains, allowing them to pursue their dreams with unwavering passion and determination. By questioning assumptions and changing perspectives, they unlock their potential. Achieve remarkable outcomes.

4. Overcoming the Scarcity Mentality: The scarcity mentality fosters fear, lack and limitation, trapping individuals in a cycle of constraint and insufficiency. Those with the Mindset of breaking free reject scarcity and instead embrace abundance, prosperity and possibility. They nurture a mindset of abundance by recognizing their value and the boundless opportunities that await them.

5. Rising Above Challenges: The Mindset of breaking free empowers individuals to conquer every obstacle that obstructs their path. Whether it's fear, failure or adversity, they confront challenges with bravery and resilience, refusing to let them hinder their journey towards success.

They perceive obstacles as stones towards greatness, learning from setbacks and emerging even stronger than before.

6. Embracing Opportunities with Enthusiasm: Lastly, the "Get Out" Mindset involves embracing opportunities with enthusiasm and determination. Instead of waiting for success to come their way, individuals with this Mindset proactively pursue their goals with passion and determination. They take risks, make decisions and refuse to let fear hinder them from achieving their dreams.

In summary, the "Get Out" Mindset is an approach that empowers individuals to break free from their comfort zones, thinking patterns, self-limiting beliefs, scarcity mentality and any other hurdles that stand in the way of success. They unlock their potential by embracing change, overcoming obstacles, and seizing opportunities. Create a life filled with fulfilment, abundance and positive impact.

***

Action Mindset

****

The "Action Mindset" concept revolves around being proactive and driven to achieve desired outcomes. It emphasizes overcoming procrastination, indecision and fear by taking steps towards our goals. Those who adopt an action mindset are motivated by purpose, determination and a willingness to step outside their comfort zones to pursue their dreams.

1. Setting Goals and Planning Strategically: The Action Mindset starts with establishing measurable objectives. It involves conducting analyses setting SMART (Specific, Measurable, Achievable, Relevant, Time-bound) goals and outlining steps to move closer to those goals.

2. Taking Initiatives: Individuals with an Action Mindset promptly initiate action plans once they have set their goals and developed plans. They utilize project management methodologies such as Agile or Six Sigma to break down tasks into portions, allocate resources effectively and establish timelines for execution.

3. Managing Risks and Implementing Mitigation Strategies: A crucial aspect of the Action Mindset is recognizing risks that may arise along the way. Those with this Mindset proactively implement strategies to mitigate these risks effectively. This includes conducting risk assessments, identifying challenges, and creating plans to minimize project timelines and goal disruptions.

4. Tracking and Control Measures: People with an Action Mindset use tracking and control measures to monitor progress, identify any deviations from the plan, and take necessary actions using Key Performance Indicators (KPIs); regular progress meetings with yourself to ensure alignment with goal objectives.daily self-talk and treating your goal as the project is essential in an action mindset.

5. Continuous Improvement and Adaptation: The Action Mindset emphasizes a culture of improvement and adaptation. Individuals regularly evaluate daily performance, gather self-feedback, and implement lessons learned to enhance processes and optimize results. This iterative approach promotes agility and responsiveness in the face of changing circumstances.

6. Self-Resource Optimization and Efficiency: Efficiency and Self-resource optimization are aspects of the

Action Mindset. Individuals prioritize tasks based on their impact on goal objectives, allocate resources wisely and streamline processes to reduce waste while maximizing productivity. This may involve adopting methodologies or utilizing a resource management cheat sheet (smart bro code) for resource allocation.

7. Documentation and Knowledge Management: Effective documentation and knowledge management are elements of the Action Mindset. Individuals maintain records of goal activities, decisions made, and outcomes achieved to facilitate knowledge transferability while ensuring continuity of operations. This involves recording and sharing insights, practical methods, and established procedures to guide goals and improve the overall knowledge within the self (here, the self is referred to as mind/manas).

Simply put, the Action Mindset embodies a deliberate method for accomplishing goals. It involves planning, proactive implementation, risk assessment and mitigation, ongoing enhancements, resource optimization, and thorough documentation. Embracing this Mindset allows individuals to excel in achieving goals, attaining desired results and adding value to their professional pursuits.

NOTE: Action Mindset I am trying to integrate a company workflow into a self-individual and treat oneself as an organization, taking methodological action and trying to make things automated to achieve the goal objective.

***

Epilogue

As we conclude our exploration into the ten mindsets, it becomes evident that our Mindset influences our experiences and shapes the collective reality we create together. Each Mindset offers a viewpoint. Set of principles for navigating life's complexities empowering us to overcome obstacles, embrace opportunities and live with intention and purpose.

From the Growth Mindset that encourages us to see challenges as chances for growth to the Abundance Mindset that cultivates gratitude and a sense of abundance, the valuable insights and strategies presented in this book hold transformative power. By developing resilience, taking action and embracing change with bravery and certainty, we can unlock our potential and build a life filled with significance, contentment and influence.

As you contemplate the lessons learned and insights gained from this journey, I invite you to integrate the wisdom of these ten mindsets into your life. Let them serve as guiding principles as you navigate challenges and opportunities, allowing them to empower you to live with purpose, enthusiasm, and resilience. Remember that within yourself lies the ability to transform your life; armed with the Mindset, everything becomes possible.

Embrace the adventure, have faith in your skills and allow your Mindset to guide you towards a future brimming with opportunities and potential.

We will meet in Volume 2…………..…

With appreciation and optimism

[*Globetrotting_Urban Saint*]

***

48 days Challenge

Days 1-7: Embrace Growth Mindset

Day 1: Take a moment to reflect on your Mindset. Are there any areas in your life that could benefit from adopting a growth mindset?

Days 2-4: Identify one challenge or goal that you've been avoiding out of fear of failure. Break it down into more manageable tasks.

Days 5-7: Take action on one of these daily tasks. Embrace any mistakes or setbacks as opportunities for learning and personal growth.

Days 8-14: Learn from Failure

Day 8: Jot down three setbacks or failures you've experienced. Reflect on the lessons you can learn from each of these experiences.

Days 9-12: Choose an area where you've encountered failure and devise a plan to give it another try, incorporating the lessons learned.

Days 13-14: Put your plan into action. Embrace any setbacks along the way as feedback. Adjust your approach accordingly.

Days 15-21: Persistence and Resilience

Day 15: Choose a long-term objective that requires determination and the ability to bounce back from setbacks.

Days 16-19: Break down your objective into milestones. Create a timeline for achieving each one.

Days 20-21: Commit to consistently take action towards your objective every day for the week. Keep track of your progress. Celebrate small accomplishments along the way.

Days 22-28: Seeking Feedback and Constructive Criticism

Day 22: Reach out to a trusted friend, mentor or colleague. Ask for their feedback on a project or endeavour.

Days 23-25: Reflect on the feedback you receive. Identify areas where you can improve and develop a plan to address them.

Days 26-28: Apply your feedback to your work or project. Embrace criticism as an opportunity for growth and improvement.

Days 29-35: Recognizing Effort and Progress

Day 29: Take time to acknowledge and celebrate your achievements, no matter how small.

Days 30-33: Dedicate some time each day to reflect upon your progress towards your goals. Jot down three things that you take pride in accomplishing.

Days 34-35: Treat yourself to something as a reward for your hard work and commitment.

Days 36-42: Nurturing an Abundance Mindset

Day 36: Cultivate gratitude by writing down three things you feel grateful for daily.

Days 37-39: Challenge yourself to adopt a mindset across all aspects of your life. Identify areas where you may be caught up in a scarcity mentality and shift your perspective accordingly.

Days 40-42: Take steps to manifest abundance in your life. Whether exploring opportunities, fostering relationships or investing in growth, embrace the abundance surrounding you.

Days 43-48: Embracing an Action-oriented Mindset

Day 43: Set a goal. Challenge yourself in a way that resonates with your values and aspirations.

Days 44-46: Develop a plan to achieve your goal by breaking it down into steps with specific deadlines.

Days 47-48: Taking steps and following through with your plan is essential. Don't allow fear or doubt to hinder your progress. Believe in yourself. Stay dedicated until you achieve your goal.

During this 48-day journey, add a new shield every day and practice the day 1 task till day 48. Go on adding tasks mentioned from 1-48, and remind yourself to stay focused on growth and progress. Embrace challenges as chances for learning and self-improvement. Always remember that to grow something new, you need to let go of something old, clear space to occupy something good, remove all the things that are making you weak, and remove it for once and all. Don't forget to acknowledge and celebrate the milestones along the way. With the Mindset and unwavering determination, there's no limit to what you can accomplish.

***

Note